KNOW YOURSELF
SANGUINE

ALEX CARBERRY

To my mother
Ruth Carberry
&
in memory of
my father-in-law
Frank Spooner
& my uncle
Godfrey Wilmott King

Copyright

Know Yourself: Sanguine

© Alexander Carberry 2015
First Edition published by Bahr Press

Published by: Alex Carberry –
287 Blackpool Street
Burton-upon-Trent,
Staffordshire,
DE14 3AR,
United Kingdom

Website: www.alexcarberry.net

Email: info@alexcarberry.net

Written by: Alexander Carberry
General Editor: Jeremy Rowland
Cover photograph: © Baraka Carberry 2010
Cover Design: Khadijah Carberry

A catalogue record of this book is available from the British Library.

ISBN-13: 978-0-9564513-2-3

ABOUT THE AUTHOR

Alex Carberry was born in London England and was raised in Guyana South America on the edge of the Amazon. He returned to the United Kingdom to study , but after meeting with a Sufi teacher chose instead to embark upon the Sufic path. He has since spent over 20 years studying Sufism, philosophy, natural medicine, geo-politics and Daoist martial arts. He is a practicing herbalist and resides in Burton-upon-Trent, England.

CONTENTS

PREFACE

BY SHAYKH ABDALHAQQ BEWLEY

One of the most unwarranted axioms of the age we live in is the arrogant claim that the human race is now at its highest-ever point of evolution, with the inevitable corollary that everything in the past, before this time, was in some way inferior to what exists in the present. This is especially prevalent in the arena of the natural sciences, and even seems somehow justifiable in the light of the plethora of dazzling technical advances achieved during the last century or so in every field of scientific research. What is not taken into account, however, when viewing things in this way, is the fact that all this has only been made possible by the millennia of human endeavor that lie behind it and have made it possible.

Modern man seems to think that all these modern inventions and discoveries came virtually out of nowhere but the truth is that they have been entirely dependent on foundations laid down far in the past. The whole history of science can be seen graphically as taking the form of an exponential curve: for the first 98% of its trajectory the line of the curve scarcely seems to move upwards at all and then suddenly it shoots up almost vertically to the top of the graph. But the final dramatic escalation is entirely contingent on the very lengthy period of apparent stasis that preceded it.

Nowhere is this attitude more explicitly articulated than in the field of medicine. It is as if the reductionist, modern approach to the treatment of illness with its microscopically precise analysis of the human anatomy and the nature of the diseases that afflict it, together with the drugs that have been chemically engineered to counteract them, and various mechanical procedures and devices that have been developed to assist it, are the only possible valid means to the restoration of good health in the human being. All previous theories of medicine, stretching back through the millennia of human history, practised by countless generations of human beings in many clearly sophisticated civilisations in every part of the world, are now considered to be at best inspired guesswork and at worst (and more often) ignorant superstition.

Distinguished recent research into the history of human intellectual development has shown that human brainpower in fact reached the zenith of its potency at some point during the first millennium BC, in other words almost three thousand years ago, and has, if anything been slightly on the decline ever since. It is patently absurd to suggest that the human race at the height of its mental capacity would have chosen to adhere to any medical system that did not, in both theory and practice, meet the requirements demanded of it. In fact it is clear that the therapeutic regimes of that age were far more concerned with, and successful at, keeping people in a state of good health and preventing illness from occurring than in having to treat them once they became unwell. As a savant said in the last century, "If someone were to be transported from ancient times to the present, they would not be so much amazed at the sophisticated techniques of modern medicine as horrified at the appalling state of modern health!"

And this brings me directly to the book, to which these words are acting as a somewhat unworthy introduction. Alexander Carberry is an experienced therapist who bases his medical practice on perhaps the most ancient of all medical theories: Humourism or the Theory of the Four Humours. I am not qualified to speak with any authority about this theory but this is a brief outline of its basic principles. It holds that there are four fundamental elements – earth, water, fire and air. The human body contains four humours that connect with these elements: blood, which connects with air and is hot and wet; yellow bile, which connects with fire and is hot and dry; black bile, which connects with earth and is cold and dry; and phlegm, which connects with water and is cold and wet. The domination of one of these humours within someone's body leads to that person being of one of four basic temperamental types:

Red – blood – sanguine;
Yellow – bile – choleric;
Black – bile – melancholic;
and White – phlegm – phlegmatic.

Good health is achieved when, according to the particular temperament of the person concerned, the correct balance between the four humours is restored and maintained. Hippocrates, to whom this theory of medicine is often ascribed, expressed it thus:

> "The Human body contains blood, phlegm, yellow bile and black bile. These are the things that make up its constitution and cause its sickness and health. Health is primarily that state in which these constituent substances are in the correct proportion to each other, both in strength and quantity, and are well mixed. Sickness occurs when one of the substances presents either a deficiency or an excess, or is separated in the body and not mixed with others."

This is the barest outline of what constitutes an extremely sophisticated and complex system of medicine, one that may well be the very bedrock on which all human medical practice was founded. Although, as I said, it is often ascribed to the ancient Greek physician, Hippocrates, who lived from 460 to 370 BC, he was only really responsible for formally systematizing it, and the fact that, to this day, all doctors still take the Hippocratic oath shows in how much respect he is still held. In fact, however, the roots of the theory he advocated stretch back far earlier in time to Ancient Egypt and Babylon and beyond. The system was taken up by the great Muslim doctor and philosopher, Avicenna, whose magnum opus The Canon of Medicine remained the chief point of reference for European doctors until well into the 18th Century. Its universality is reflected in the fact that Chinese and Indian medicine have always been clearly based on the same principles and, in their case, as evinced by Unani and Ayurvedic medicine in the Indian Subcontinent and Chinese traditional medicine in China and, indeed, in the many other countries where these systems are still employed daily and successfully by countless practitioners and patients, it is evident that Humourism is still very much alive and in use in the world today.

One of the main reasons for this is that, in contradistinction to modern allopathic medicine, which looks at and treats illnesses in a purely symptomatic way, the practitioners of Humourism treat their patients on a far more holistic basis, seeing their conditions within the totality of their individual, family, social, economic, cultural and political circumstances and examining the way that all those things affect them in the light of the own temperamental type, dictated by the humoural mix that makes up their own particular being. One result of this is that the more or less rigid line drawn by Western medicine between physical and mental illness does not exist in the Humoural system and the remedies prescribed by the doctors who adhere to it address simultaneously all the health problems faced by their patients, whether these are of a physical or psychological nature or, as is all too often the case, both at the same time.

Alexander Carberry's earlier book Know Yourself is a masterful introduction to this now sadly vastly underrated therapeutic method. I defy anyone to read it to the end and fail to recognise from it which admixture of the temperamental types – sanguine, choleric, melancholic and phlegmatic – best describe their own particular personality make-up. This subsequent volume, the first in a series of four, looks in far greater detail at just one of these, concentrating on the particular characteristics that go to form the sanguine personality, underscoring the strengths and failings that people of this nature display in their lives, and giving much practical advice to them about the ways in which those strengths may be enhanced and those failings mitigated. However, Alexander's words also open the way to something much deeper, prefigured in his basic title, Know Yourself.

There is a saying, sometimes attributed to the Prophet Muhammad himself, which goes: "He who truly knows himself, knows his Lord." In other words true self-knowledge leads the one who possesses it to direct cognition of his own source and the source of all existence and to the vast and inexpressible love and fathomless wisdom that flow from that experience. In our time the main means to knowledge of the self is thought by many to be psychoanalysis. On the psychiatrist's couch individuals look back through their lives and uncover the influences and traumas that have made them into the people they now are, enabling them, in their eyes, to achieve the self-knowledge they are searching for. What this fails to recognize is that, in this process, they are not actually looking at themselves at all; they are only looking at what has happened to themselves, what was done to themselves, what they did to themselves. What humouralism allows people to do is to look at the true nature of their own selves, at what really underlies the traumas which psychoanalysis focuses on, at what is the actual substructure of their beings, determining how they react to all the situations they face during the course of their lives. While this deeper kind of self-knowledge, derived from humoural theory, does not, of course, lead all who have it to the great unveiling I referred to, it does make it a real possibility for all those who truly desire it.

INTRODUCTION

Welcome! Well you have read Know Yourself: Discover Your True Nature with the Ancient Sufic Wisdom and know that you are a Sanguine. This book is for sanguines and for those who want more insight into this wonderful and colourful personality type. By now you will have discovered the personality types of those around you and enjoyed your accurate prediction of their antics. Is it not simply amazing? Apple trees produce apples and they do not produce pears! People are what they are and it is as if there is an invisible music to which we are all dancing on our journeys through life.

If you are just reading this book out of interest and are not a Sanguine, I promise it will be interesting. You will see that a Sanguine is a Sanguine but you will also see the vast variety which may be found within this type. That is the wonderful thing, for within these four types there is endless variety. Trees are trees but there is such variation! Apple trees are apple trees but there is such

1

variation. People usually dislike the idea that they conform to a type, they usually feel that this is limiting and simplistic, but on the contrary! Your type shows your natural energetic signature and we will see that no two Sanguines are the same despite the striking similarities that characterise Sanguines. Life is great when you are having fun and Sanguines love to have fun. A Sanguine is a Sanguine and that is just the way they are wired.

Sanguine is a Sanguine

As a Sanguine you are in harmony with the Element Air. The wind is very similar to you, it picks things up and drives them along, bringing movement and change as it moves along. It changes direction often, connecting things which are separate by sound and smell. Your energetic signature and purpose is very similar. The season you are in harmony with is Spring and so you are like the spring. The spring bursts forth bringing life, growth and change. Like spring you are colourful, free, fresh, bringing birth, activity and delight. It's a wonderful type to be. Though sanguines vary much, they all love communicating, telling exciting stories and bringing colour to our social lives. This underlying harmony is instructive to sanguines, for it shows the secret of your purpose, revealing your natural strengths and inherent weaknesses. Being Sanguine is wonderful, for sanguines love delight and what we love is what we attract. In this book we will really explore sanguines and the various sanguine combinations. I promise that you will discover more about yourself than you bargained for. We will really study the biological occurrence that is the sanguine. Some things will be comfortable and a joy to know and of course some will be uncomfortable; but we are human and sanguines are not new to the Earth. You should know that sanguines have been facing the challenges that you face since mankind began. We can all get a handle of being ourselves and have a load of fun whilst dealing with the challenges, but as Johan von Goethe said, 'If God had wanted me otherwise, He would have created me otherwise.

'You are a Sanguine and that is just the way you are wired!

Apple Trees Do Not Produce Bananas

Yes apple trees do not produce bananas, we all know that. People ask me if they can or will change type, looking dejected when I tell them that this is just the way they are. They find this very difficult to come to terms with. This is despite the fact that they accept that an apple will never become a banana and neither shall a banana become an apple. In the world there are some things that we always treat according to their natures, however we would desperately like ourselves to be the exception. We are just what we are and rather than this limiting us, it gives us a fixed form with which to work. We may mould, change and transform ourselves but we are working with the same basic pattern material. The energetic signature that we are, will continue to be expressed in endless ways. You will always recognise a Beethoven symphony, or Wagner or Brahms. We will always recognise Ella Fitzgerald, Whitney Houston or Amy Winehouse. There is a clear signature. We are all like that. There is a music singing through us. It sings in our DNA, our voices and the sound of our steps. It characterises us. We smell of it, are it and those that love us love it. It probably means that those that hate us also hate it, but who said that we were here to please everyone. This is just the way we are. It is our song and no one else's. There are of course endless things that we can change, develop and strengthen but our unique energetic signature will remain the same. You are you! You can be no other! As Desiderius Erasmus said, 'It is the chiefest point of happiness that a man is willing to be what he is.'. Wise words! Wise words indeed.

So you are what you are and your personality type is a description of the energetic signature of your psyche, which is from the Greek for breath, its Sufic equivalent is the Arabic word ruh, which is from breath also. The Greek and Arabic words psyche and ruh both mean soul. So what I am saying is that, what you are witnessing with the knowledge of personality types is the very patterning of souls. Apple trees do not produce bananas and that is just the way it is.

The Forest and the Trees

A personality type is like a forest of pine fir trees. Though all the pine fir trees are similar and from the same family of tree. Every one of them is unique. Amongst them are groups of trees that possess similar traits. By the end of this book I will show you the various different types of sanguines and how they differ.

What Will You Get From This Book

You will learn about Sanguines, more about Sanguines and even more about Sanguines. Which should not be surprising because this is a book about Sanguines. If you want the indepth details about the other types then read the other books:

Know Yourself: Choleric;
Know Yourself: Melancholic;
and Know Yourself: Phlegmatic.

They will do the same with the other personality types. But this book will only be about Sanguines. We will be able to begin to develop the ability to take a look at ourselves in a way similar to the manner in which an artist may look at a painting, with attention to the details, seeing the brushstrokes, the hues, tones and richness of colour. We will look at the proportions, the composition and the perspective. Then you will be able to say this is a Da Vinci, a Van Gogh or a Gaugin. You will develop the art of seeing the texture of your own personality and this is the same skill you will utilise to examine others. You will develop a remarkable ability to see the texture of people. This skill will be yours forever and you will be able to use it to understand your greatest wealth which is your own self.

By getting to know yourself, you will learn to know others. Now how is that for efficiency!

You will also gain some tips on dealing with yourself and the aspects of your personality that you may find difficult. I will even give you some tips on how to use the difficult aspects to your advantage.I will also give you more of an insight into your genius. That is using the word genius in it original Latin sense of 'your natural inclination or natural abilities'. Yes you are a genius and there is not another genius like you anywhere on the planet. I intend to help you on the journey to discovering that.You will begin to discover how to play to your genius and how to avoid the areas in which you are naturally weak. You will learn that once you enter into an area in which you are naturally weak, then you should have a plan and some techniques to keep or get you out of trouble. For those who are not Sanguines, I might just give you some tips on dealing with difficult Sanguines. I just might but do remember that this is a book for Sanguines and they may not be happy about me giving these tips away, but I might do so nonetheless.I will stop listing the things I intend to give. If there is anything that would be of benefit to you, I intend to share it. I want you to be the best that you can be. I intend to give you as much as I possibly can. This series is to be designed to be short and easy to read, you should be able to read one of these books quickly and easily. So within those limits I will share with you as much as I possibly can.

Let Others Be What They Are

If you are not convinced that people are just the way they are because they are wired that way, then I suspect that by the end of this book it will become much more difficult for you to hold onto the idea that human beings are like plastic and can be moulded in any way that we like. Calling it evolution or whatsoever else you choose to call the desire to make a thing what it is not, will not change the truth of what people are. We are what we are. When we accept that we are as we are and get on with the job of dealing with ourselves, then we will give ourselves the permission to allow others to be as they are. We do not have to make them into clones of ourselves or someone else. We have to let ourselves and others be what and who we all are. We can strengthen natural strengths, find strategies to deal with natural weaknesses and thank God we can tell each other off for the bad habits. But remember we are what we are and if you desire to make a lion out of an elephant then good luck to you. I will bet upon the odds that you will fail! What is worse is that it is a tyranny upon ourselves and upon others, to try to force ourselves and each other to be what we are not, and it is impossible as many continue to discover.

Who Should Read This Book

Read this book if you have read 'Know Yourself: Discover Your True Nature with the Ancient Sufic Wisdom', which is the first book in the series, or you have read another book on personality types which has helped you to be certain about what your personality type is. If you are reading this book you should be a Sanguine or interested in finding out about Sanguines.

How To Read This Book

Go through the contents pages, and as you go, stop and take a quick look at anything that strikes your attention. This will stimulate your interest, provide you with an overview of the structure of the book, as well as encourage you to read it. It may also be helpful to read the book quickly once through. Things are easier to understand and remember if they are in context. After reading through once, than return to the parts that you feel necessary to re-read and reflect on.

Discuss some of the concepts with those around you. One of the easiest ways to learn and remember is to share what you know. Question those who have known you for a long time about the way that they see you. Observe carefully the way you and others do things. Remember, you do not have to like something for it to be true. Some truths are bitter to begin with, but that is their sweetness, for things can only be what they are and the energy spent in trying to make things what they are not, is certainly energy wasted. You will discover much about yourself that you like and much that you do not. What we are working towards is not liking what we see, but surrendering to the truth or reality of things as they are. Redness does not change because we may dislike it!

We may change the shade, tone and hue of red but redness always remains redness. Our fundamental nature is analogous to colouring in this respect. So, read the book, make your observations and once they become truly clear to you, accept them. Remember, the stories that we tell ourselves about ourselves and about everything else, are just stories; the way things really are transcends our stories. Over time our dislike and resistance to the way things are will change to acceptance and we will be free to work with what is there, rather than attempting to maintain an illusion. Over time and with practice our need to persist with our stories in the face of reality diminishes.

Welcome to the Journey

If you have made it this far then congratulations. Let us continue the journey further into the depths of our personality type, to discover the treasures, discoveries and wonders. I continue to be fascinated by this knowledge and am really excited about sharing it with you. I hope that you will be even more excited and fascinated than I have been and I pray that you will enjoy it even more than I have.

The amazing thing about the Universe is that just the act of discovering something new, which means that you know something new, means that the entire Universe itself has changed. Everything is changing, yet everything remains the same. Transformation is in the very nature of the Universe and you are not separate from it. You were born to be what you are and to be the best that you can be.

Will the reward of doing good be anything other than good?
So which of the favours of your Lord do you both deny?
The Noble Qur'an: 55:60 - 61

THE PURE SANGUINE

She stood there chatting, as if holding court. Her head held pertly, her lively eyes dancing in delight at the reactions of the audience, they held onto her every word. Laughter and joy engulfed her company. Her expressions and hands told the stories in ways that went beyond words. She was the life of the party. Yes! She is one of us! A sanguine a real sanguine!

Description of the Sanguine

The Sanguine possesses natural social intelligence, you pick things up in the air, you smell them and taste them as a deer sniffs and tastes its surroundings. Sanguines sense the way people are with a natural intelligence driven by intuition. You love to tell stories and to communicate and usually it is most enjoyable when you are doing most of the talking, since you are very good at doing the talking. Sanguines are talkers, its part of your impulse. You tell wonderful stories. Sanguines are expressive and deeply communicative. You love life and like to enjoy the journey much more than you enjoy arriving at the goal. You are flexible and love change as long as it allows the expression of your deep impulses. There is a strong need to be expressive and to keep your options open. You do not like to be boxed in. You are passionate, loving and generous. Sanguines are good at using their social intelligence to get their own way because they do not like to be boxed in. If there is one statement that describes the nature of the Sanguine it is that you are 'the life of the party'.

The Sanguine in Action

You are at a dinner party and in comes Patrick, he is casually dressed or at least has some dash of colour or expression that marks him out from the crowd. He walks confidently as if he believes that the world is in love with him (and it probably is), he draws attention to himself effortlessly, it is as if he did so without even trying (and most likely he didn't. At least he did not try too hard). Patrick seems to know everyone, even if he cannot remember their names. He seems to know everyone intimately and can engage them all in conversation. He makes his rounds greeting everyone, occasionally he may say the wrong thing but he gets away with it by sheer charisma and overwhelming charm. He finds himself a corner and soon surrounds himself with an audience as he tells story after story, anyone in the crowd who produces another story, you can be sure that dear Patrick has a better one. What a sight it is when there are a few Sanguines in Patrick's group then the stories become wilder, more embellished and oh so funny. They all laugh and chat and Patrick continues, it is as if the conversation and company fill him with energy, and he loves being the centre of attention. He will entertain at one hundred miles per hour, without any need of breaks. It is as if he was made for this (and he is).

Patrick loves to communicate and if the company turns out to be a really boring group, Patrick will either raise the tempo by his entertainment or he will flee like a bee in search of nectar.

This is a description of a very strong Sanguine in whom we can see very little evidence of the other elements or personality types. Some of this, if not all of it, will probably ring true for you.

The World According to a Sanguine

Let us imagine a sanguine describing themselves. It is probably a CV or an interview:

I have lots of friends and am a very friendly person. People generally like me and I them. I am really a peoples person and really like people. I love entertaining and conversing. People find my company enjoyable and I love to be with them. I tell wonderful stories and jokes. I am also very creative and love to bring new ideas and invent new things. I hate repetitive tasks and love variation and new challenges. When I do something I want it to be colourful, engaging and fun.

Things I Hate

As I said I hate repetitive tasks, finding them boring and pointless. I cannot stand a group that doesn't want to talk and to have fun. I hate doing the same things and so need lots of variety in my life. Being boxed in and not having my freedom to change and keep my options open is stifling. I love flexibility. I hate the embarrassing silences that occur when I have said something inappropriate but know how to move on quickly from them, it is part of life and though I wish it did not happen, it sometimes does and so what, it certainly does make life interesting. I hate it when people misread my intentions. Death and sickness are among my pet hates and I tend to deal with really awkward situations by running away or avoiding them, since I hate awkward situations.

My Outlook

Life is wonderful, it should be fun and there should be variety. I do not do boring or routine well and will do my best to avoid them. If work is not fun it is deadly. I love to win arguments but really prefer to move on rather than to battle over a pointless one. In a conversation silences are awkward and it is better to say something rather than to let everyone suffer the silences.

The Sanguine According to the Rest of the World

The Good Points

It's really useful to be able to see yourself through others eyes. It can make all the difference. Usually everyone enjoys sanguines for their amazing social intelligence. This makes them lovable, for the sake of space and also to prevent the sanguine ego from becoming over-inflated, I will not repeat all of their good qualities. Sanguines make life interesting for all the reasons that we have looked at before. They are thick skinned and do not become offended easily. Even when they do react, do not expect it to last for very long. Sanguines are dramatic and they come across as such, we all expect sanguines to overdramatise things. The two cats fighting in the garden becomes a great battle of wildlife akin to an epic battle of timeless heroes. They make a wonderful story out of anything. Sanguines provide lots of ideas and other ways of seeing things. They are usually so active and colourful that they develop a following. We love the company of Sanguines it makes life so interesting.

The Complaints

Sanguines Love to talk! They never stop talking. Sanguines talk and talk. They can be so caught up in the pleasure of their stories that they will not let you leave. If we want to visit a sanguine we have got to give it lots of time. They are so convinced that they are fun, that they can become oblivious to any lack of interest or boredom. If they realise our lack of interest or boredom, they are likely to be off in a flash (without even being upset) to alight upon a new victim and if you are the only one available then may heaven help you!

Sanguines are unreliable! Sanguines change their minds often, lose interest and change direction like the wind. When we have planned our lives around the Sanguine and they change direction, we have got to pick up the pieces and sanguines tend to do this often. Since you do not like to do 'boring' and since anything that is not fun is avoided other people end up saddled with the 'boring' jobs. It is an irritant and we pay for the colour and life you bring to the party.

Sanguines have lots of ideas, especially hare-brained ones! You change direction and lines of thought often. You generate many ideas, looking at many possibilities and since you know what you are thinking by expressing it, or we may say you think by doing (talking, drawing, exploring and writing, etc.), you let us know about it all without discrimination. Some of the ideas are very good but we have got to listen to all of them, including the many hare-brained ones. This is what sometimes causes some of us to roll our eyes when you come up with ideas. You look at angles that we would discount as utterly impractical and you explore them, it seems to us that exploration and creativity are more important to you than practicality and some of us practical types just find this all a bit too much to stomach so often.

Sanguines are insensitive! You say the most insensitive things at times, often in the wrong context, to the wrong people and often at the wrong time. It does not seem to bother you and sometimes you just cannot keep a secret. You will blurt out the most inappropriate things and will often just move on after a theatrical gasp or flare up and will definitely do it again. The more sensitive types amongst us assume that you have really thought it through and sometimes will take your slip of the tongue or putting your foot in it, in ways you never intended. We may feel insulted, betrayed or deeply hurt but you sanguine, will just move on skipping gaily along to do it all again, repeatedly.

Everything is a drama with a Sanguine! Your attachment to the theatrical means that you overdramatise, embellish and inflate every story and circumstance. If I burnt the dinner, I was burning the kitchen down. If you had an accident on the motorway anyone would believe that it was the mother of all accidents. If your baby starts talking you would have us all believe that they gave the professorial inaugural lecture at the local university! You inflate everything and really need to learn to get a grip on reality. And oh as for the truth! Well that is really elastic and relative to the story you are telling, there seems to be many truths for you.

Sanguines really need to stop embellishing the truth! We have to take your stories with a pinch of salt. You embellish them with such ease and with such frequency that when we have taken part in the incident which you are relating, we begin to doubt whether we took part in the same incident. We do not believe you lie (well some of you do!), but at the very least you see the truth as something elastic and the elasticity of the truth depends upon how much you perceive your audience enjoys the story.

You are so emotional! You smother us with your kindness and attention. We all probably have a memory of a sanguine aunt who loved us to death. Smothering us with pinches, hugs, gifts, treats, stories, love and attention until all we wished to do was run away but whilst she was there, there was nowhere to hide. You will cry and laugh in the same conversation and laugh and cry in the other. Your intensity can sometimes be overwhelming and you seem to feel obligated to serve it all up in double portions whether we like it or not.

Ok I'll stop now, but I've more, alot more complaints. Oh and of a sanguine wife or husband, well do not get me started if you think I was complaining with those points, you would end up with a book thrice this size.

What a list! I can easily double its length. But that is not the point. The point is that all of the things that are our strengths have a flip side and they may become our weaknesses. Wisdom is learning what to do and when. The wise read the situation understanding where they see it going or ought to go and draw upon their natural skills to help it to happen. If we just act in a default manner with everything we will end up responding inappropriately. We need wisdom, not ideals and default behaviour. Default behaviour and ideals are blind. Wisdom allows to observe what is happening and to draw upon our knowledge and experience to do what is appropriate. Most of the complaints arise from behaving in a default manner or responding to some ideals that we may have formed in our minds. If we are blind to what is happening in front of us we will act blindly and if any of you would place your lives in the hands of a blind marksman then I believe you need your heads examined and if you do not you probably will soon lose your heads anyway. Acting blindly is like being a blind marksman, you have an amazing personality and natural gifts so learn to use them well. There is so much you can do and bring about, you have just got to learn to use what you are well.

You the Sanguine are a force of nature, like spring you bring life, birth and change. You just have to be in harmony with the meaning and purpose of your energetic impulse and that is a lifetime of work, effort and practice.

Spot the Sanguine

You can tell a Sanguine as soon as you see them, the frequent lively gestures, expressive faces and colourful elaborate stories are a dead giveaway. They love life and living, delight in fine food and must be the centre of attention. When you see these qualities in a person, you have found a true Sanguine, sit back and enjoy the show! There will definitely be entertainment and the Sanguine will be the entertainer.

Spot the Sanguine - From Know Yourself: Discover Your True Nature with the Ancient Sufic Wisdom.

So Why Are You Like This?

You are like the wind and spring. What characterises spring characterises you: liveliness, fluidity and energy. Like spring's is a time of birdsong, budding and growth. You are like that, you like to grow, move and express the potential within yourself and things. Your movements are a dead giveaway. You have open expressive movements when you gesticulate with your hands or talk with your body. You usually stand in an open and welcoming manner (people who are not like this can misread the welcoming open manner). You also tend to sit in this way. That is just the music that resounds through you. But you have to learn to understand that music and the way others may hear it. The colder more introverted types are not this welcoming so your signals may confuse them, remember context makes many things clear. Think about it.

Your stories are like the joy and promise of spring they also possess this signature. Now that we know this, we must learn how to use this inner music and 'sanguine language'. You possess it. It is your genius. Use it and use it well. All your life you will study it and it will always reveal new possibilities and insights. Being sanguine is a life adventure so enjoy the journey and delight in it. If you try to make your self development too much like work, you will most likely self sabotage. Just work with the way you are and make things interesting and fun, however there are some things which are just repetitive and hard uninteresting work and since you naturally dislike this then you have got to work out strategies for tricking yourself and making things interesting but the repetitive boring work, sometimes just has got to be done in order to move onto the more interesting.

Sanguine Relationships

In relationships you are generous, unless of course you are so self absorbed that you cannot notice the needs of the other. Sanguines are naturally generous and forgiving. You love, give and you have lots of stamina and passion. The problem that sanguines sometimes have in relationships is that since this is a default quality, they may not look closely to see what is really appropriate. Sometimes it is appropriate to give and sometimes it is appropriate to withhold, sometimes withholding is giving and giving is withholding. Sanguines have trouble grasping this truth. So I will explain it.

For example, sometimes someone needs to move on and discover something for themselves. As a sanguine your default is to help them and offer advice. You Have got to observe where they are. If they are in the condition that requires that they move on to discover things for themselves, then you must shut up and allow that to happen. Forget about what they say, look at what they do. If you see that speaking to them or helping them will not help them to do what they need to do (since they have got to work it out for themselves, in order to progress) then helping them is not really helping them, we are in reality holding them back. Advice in this case is useless because it prevents them from discovering for themselves. Then the best thing to do is to leave them alone and if we must converse then we talk about other things. In this case giving is withholding and withholding is giving.

Sanguines are generous and expect gratitude or reciprocation. If there is anything that a sanguine finds truly upsetting it is when their generosity serially receives neither gratitude, love nor reciprocation. They are just wired that way. This is part of the human struggle to give without expecting anything in return and that is difficult. However what is desired is not idealism, we cannot give at all times without expecting a return, this is done when it's appropriate. In business we expect a profit, we give something and expect something in return. However in relationships there are times when we must give and not expect anything in return, in fact the response may be just the opposite a kick in the teeth, which we are forced to endure with patience. There are also times when we must give and expect something back and it would be inappropriate to keep on giving when there is no reciprocity. There are other types who are not as naturally generous and so they must learn the opposite of what the sanguine must learn. That is just the way things are and of course thank God you do not have to deal with their side of the problem, you are just afflicted with the Sanguine side. Thank God!

In relationships you have got to learn to listen, not just to words but with your intuition and you are gifted in that way. You Have got to listen so that you 'hear' what is happening with the person. Since you are prone to making snap decisions, you really need to listen and hear before you commit to a course of action. As you listen more, more is revealed so listen and hear with your spirit. You cannot respond appropriately if you do not know what is really going on. Sanguines usually find this difficult and exhausting, so learn to take breaks, to be gracious and smart about it. Getting a cup of tea, going off to the toilet or some other ruse will do. Do not make the break long enough to destroy the flow but take them so that you can manage the interaction. You are the way you are so work with it and do not kill yourself in the process of being a good companion. This skill will help you to deal with alot of the difficulties that sanguines have. Work hard at this one.

When Sanguines commit because of their natural generosity they possess incredible stamina and will move the world. Listen carefully and hear what is going on before you commit and remember that you will make lots of mistakes, but without them we would learn very little.

Sanguines speak out of turn and tend to inadvertently give up secrets. Learn to keep secrets even from yourself. When someone tells you something in confidence learn to lock it away visualise it, put lots of locks on it and learn to steer away from the things that tempt you to speak about those things. When you sense that someone is trying to get you to reveal someone else's secret, change the subject or find an excuse to remove yourself from their company. Better still since you may be bad at keeping secrets avoid listening to them, you cannot accidentally let slip that which you do not know! Box clever and remember that boxing requires alot of practice.

Sanguines do not like to be boxed in, you feel pressure to keep your options open. In relationships do not allow yourself to boxed into commitments that you know you cannot keep, for when the windy aspect of you becomes dominant you will create a hurricane to get out of them. In hindsight you may then discover that the reason you thought the problem came along is not the one which caused you to act in the way that you did, you just felt stifled and cornered and that is not a good place for a sanguine to be. In relationships keep your options open, do not box yourself in or allow yourself to be boxed in. Of course one has to commit to things and to others or there would be no relationships. Commitment must offer us something, even if it is just loyalty and friendship; two of the most precious commodities in the world. Do not agree to things that you know you cannot keep to, for the pressure will mount and mount and one day the valve will go. Then who knows what will happen?

Ostrich Strategy Head in the Sand

Beware of the favourite sanguine strategy for dealing with pressured situations, which is to stick one's head in the sand in the hope that the problem will go away. Though the problem may well go away, you will end up with circumstances which really are not of your choosing. Dealing with things in this manner reduces your options boxing you in.

Sanguine In Love

Sanguines in love shine! They love to be loved. They love to pet, to be physical and affectionate. Some types do not like this but sanguines do. Hurrah! Sanguines are passionate lovers and give up everything, they love deeply and trust. Sanguines give their whole hearts. Sometimes the extent of sanguine love can be overwhelming, so a sanguine must learn to listen and to 'hear' and not to smother. Your capacity for stories can engulf you and so you may tell a fairytale about your love. You must listen and 'hear' and learn to distinguish between your stories and what is really happening. You will want to give so completely that you are blinded, give but hold something back so that you can see. Often it is impossible to do so, but the awareness of its necessity can help you to see, listen and hear what is occurring.

Sanguines are sensuous, passionate and inventive. They are also curious.

Sanguines love to receive gifts and romantic gestures. They like confirmation of love in touches, eye contact and communication of the fact that they are mutually in love. This is their love language. They need it. Too much of it however may eventually become stifling even for the sanguine. I mentioned this because I know that this is the section that other types will tend to turn to. You are usually attracted to your opposite. It is a principle of the universe that opposites attract. I often see sanguines and melancholics together, they complement each other but usually have some difficulties. Once they are married, they forget why they were attracted to the other in the first place. The project becomes the transformation of the other into a clone of themselves and this frustrating, unrewarding and pointless warfare, is usually the driver of much strife in marriages and relationships.

A heartbroken Sanguine is cut deeply. It is as if the hurt goes to the foundations of the earth. Avoid the temptation to move on in an attempt to hide from the pain. The pain is a wound and despite how painful it may be it will heal with time. An old injury will often remind you of its presence and a broken heart is like that, there are times when it will remind you but that is a necessary part of living and learning how to heal will make you a stronger and better person. Give the wound time to heal or you may find yourself jumping from relationship to relationship in an attempt to hide from the pain of a broken heart. You have an amazing capacity to be superficial and to move on. It will not work in fact it will most likely make the problem worse with time. Let the natural processes happen. Let the healing take its course. The problem is that recovering from a broken heart is difficult for you because sanguines do not really like to be alone. This is a time to search your thoughts and understand what has happened and what has caused you to do what you have done; to understand why the other person was attracted to you and what really happened in the relationship. Since you are a sanguine, take some time alone and some time with those you trust and can confide in, remember that sanguines really need to get things out to make sense of them. A diary might help.

Sanguine Friend

Well there will be fun, things will be forgotten and many times there will not be a plan. Sanguines love to play it by ear and can tend to be quite disorganised. We all tend to admire the qualities that we do not have, after all the grass is always greener on the other side, and we are attracted to our opposite, for this reason we often have friends who are quite unlike ourselves. But this is not a bad thing, for we need to support ourselves with the company and points of view that we do not have and this helps us to become more complete human beings. You will usually be the one who provides the fun, much of the ideas and entertainment. On the other hand someone has to look into the detail and worry about what could possibly go wrong; whilst another will make sure that some things get done and that we have some focus; whilst another will sit back and observe with the occasional wry smile and sense of humour (can you tell which type each of them is?). All the types are necessary to keep life interesting.

As a friend you are: loyal, forgiving, very difficult to hurt deeply, excitable, storytelling, fun, interesting, passionate, generous, have loads of ideas, a natural party seeking hound, friendly and talkative. You are loyal and generous, so make sure that you at least have some close friends that you may confide in and who will look out for your interest when you may be doing something particularly hare-brained. It tends to happen and you should protect yourself against this by having those around that you can trust implicitly and who love you and have your best interests at heart. Keep them close and maintain those relationships, they will prove to be a Godsend when difficulties come or those close to you may misunderstand you. Your true friends will seek them out when they feel that you will not listen, in the hope that someone you trust may help. You need at least one of these trusted friends. Ensure that you really understand their needs and beware of being so self absorbed that you fail to cater for them. You need friends who understand how you really are, who appreciate your inner workings and know how to approach delicate matters. Invest in them for they are worth their weight in gold.

Remember each type is what it is. Bring life to your friends lives but remember that people differ and so have the generosity to give them the space that they require.

Some helpful tips:

1) Learn to listen;

2) Give your friends space and quiet when they need it;

3) Keep the really close friends close;

4) Know what matters to your close friends;

Invest in Relationships.

If you are reading this because you have a sanguine friend who gets themselves into trouble, here is a tip, Sanguines tend to be focussed upon the present and will tend to not look too far into the future (if they do at all). It can sometimes be difficult to get them to see the consequences of their actions, perhaps a way of dealing with this is not to always be too quick and severe about pointing these things out. Point it out gently if appropriate or not at all and when the disaster happens explain to them what has happened and how. Show them some options that would have had different outcomes and add that this is why I said what I said to you. They will most likely not listen the first time, or the second, or the third, but sooner or later it will become too expensive to suffer the pain repeatedly and when you warn them they will be more prepared to listen. The day they willingly try your solution then you have won their trust do not force them, let them come to you, the wind does not like to be contained and when it is, it is no longer the wind.

Sanguine at Work

Variety, work must be fun! There must be interest and change, sanguines need to do things that involve much variety. You are very good at dealing with people so choose things that engage your great social intelligence and genius. If it doesn't engage your creativity it may prove difficult. To deal with routine tasks try these five ways of dealing with them.

Five Ways of Dealing With Routine Tasks

1) Examine the task creatively and see how you

can do it in an interesting and novel way, ensuring that the important and necessary parts of the task are well done. Imagine yourself telling stories of how you cracked this boring task, in a way that no one thought of before. Imagine yourself spicing up the story. Now when you are doing the task use this image to remind you and reward yourself by telling really roaring stories of how you did it. Maybe you might even get a chance to tell Mr and Mrs Routine how to do it better and actually have fun whilst doing so. Heehee now that would be a change!;

2) Set a reward for each stage of the task and only reward yourself after you have done it, but make a big issue of the reward;

3) Make your out breaths longer than the inward ones and dwell upon the natural pause at the end of the exhalation. This will really calm you down and give you energy. Soften the way you look out of your eyes and let your shoulders melt into your body. Work from the calm state that results and make your way through the task whilst maintaining the state of relaxation. Try it and tell me what you think;

4) Charm someone into doing it for you. Sanguines are really good at this and tend to do it often, but remember there will be a payback day and since you do not tend to see the long term implications of things, the payback may end up being alot more than you expected or are prepared to pay. Do not take this route if you do not know what the payback will be and are willing to pay its price.

5) Tell the boss you do not do routine. In which case you had better be bloody good at what you do and irreplaceable. Remember that if someone turns up who is also good and prepared to do routine then you have some competition and could quite easily be out of a job. Also those who get stuck with the routine you refuse to do, may want to get even, so do not necessarily expect them to put in a good word for you. If you work for yourself you can pay someone else to do it, but it is really worth just knowing how to do it just in case your back is up against the wall. But if you cannot pay someone else to do it. Why not learn to get those tasks done?

If you have any other solutions that you think would be useful for sanguines please send them to me I will post them on my website and if you would like me to mention you then with your permission I will even publish your note.

When and whilst a sanguine is passionate about an activity, then they will pour their lives out for it. Remember that you are human and need life-balance. Your creative pattern has huge surges and necessary lulls, avoid exhausting yourself unnecessarily and have some cut off points that you do not go beyond unless it is absolutely necessary and work out what absolutely necessary is and learn to stick to it. When you need to chase those creative urges through to the end (I know sanguines who have done over forty eight hours without a break) then ensure that you take and set aside time to rest and recover. Creativity takes alot of energy and because you do it naturally you tend not to notice how much energy it takes. Have leisure that allows you to recover and ensure you take the time to recover. You will produce your best work whilst under pressure but the stress needs to be recovered from. The failure to do so is the cause of many diseases (I promise to write a book about this). Seeing a sanguine in this mode is a thing of beauty, you cannot help but envy this natural capacity.

Sanguine at Play

Sanguines love to play we all know that. Need I say more? Save to say remember that tomorrow must come and the things that need to be done tomorrow need energy. I really do not need to tell a sanguine anything about playing except that it is necessary for sanguine sanity. So seek and find your balance.

Sanguine Creative

The sanguine creative process is an amazing thing, you reach into the abyss of potentialities and draw them out as if from the wellspring of primal possibilities, but you are not in the abyss you are pouring out the contents from its rim, it is as if you are seeing them as they emerge. You know by getting it out, do not apologise for this, educate them on what it means to be sanguine. You will pour them out and pour them out without discrimination and if they want to learn to be truly creative let them copy you. You know instinctively that it is from this raw material that a solution will come and that within the craziest idea there is the seed of something of use. Pour them out and capture them in a way that doesn't obstruct the way they come. Record them, sketch them, write them down in short hand, draw diagrams it does not really matter but get them out and learn to put enough indications to remember where you were. Let the images flow, you were born to do this. I run courses on creativity and you will find resources on my website. Pour them out do not edit them but I do not need to tell you that, you know this instinctively anyway. Keep a notebook or recorder and catch the treasures when they come.

Everyone should know sanguines are creative, they were made for this, that is the sanguine genius, let the outpouring happen and then make use of the scattered treasures, do not try to make them edit their inspiration, that will really impair their creativity. Edit them afterwards when the surge into the abyss has ended.

If you are not a sanguine and want to turbo-charge your own creativity observe sanguines in order model their creative behavior and process. Those fuzzy ideas can come up with some real gems as you probably know. You can too but you just edit much too early and you do not stand upon the lip of the abyss as easily, but practice makes perfect.

Sanguine Student

Lastminute Dot Com

Lastminute dot com tells the story of the sanguine student. Your optimism gets the better of you. So go against your instinct and set a timetable. It will be difficult at first and you will most likely abandon it but the pain of the consequences will soon teach you a few lessons and you will slowly settle into the idea although you will most likely abandon the timetable often. The structure will help you to cover ground and so when you do the inevitable catching up or revision you won't have to expend too much energy getting to or working out the place you need to be. This will of course leave you much more energy to spend having fun. So why not begin to become accustomed to timetables?

Eight Tips For Dealing With Timetables

1) Start slowly this is not your natural strength;

2) Expect to fall off the timetable horse when you do and remember how you fell off. Pay attention to what happens, then when you see

the same pattern occurring you can take a break or just be cleverer with falling off and inevitably getting back on again;

3) Be gentle with yourself;

4) Set times for things and build habits slowly, since habits can take 30 to 40 days to become set;

5) Give yourself breaks and rewards. If you do not stay on-track then do not reward yourself, but give yourself a bigger reward when you do get back on track and hit the next reward target;

6) Go to bed early and get sufficient sleep, willing takes energy and this will take bucket-loads of will;

7) Give yourself breaks and fresh air, do not punish yourself, you are a sanguine, it will most likely backfire and you will just end up rebelling;

8) Get yourself some melancholic friends, who are willing to be helpful;

Sanguine Learning and Study Style

I) You like to be flamboyant with tremendous

variation. You will notice details that interest you and love to tell stories. Make use of your natural talents and do not work against them. When studying link the interesting facts together as a story. Pepper your notes with images and things that YOU found interesting. You do not have to justify this to anyone. Build upon the framework of the story by adding more detail and imagine yourself telling it. Whilst reviewing it notice the bits that are interesting. Be flamboyant with your retelling of the story to yourself and keep reviewing the facts to keep yourself anchored to what the matter really is;

2) Go on tell the story aloud to yourself! You know you want to;

3) If you are revising in a group share your story in a really engaging way when it is appropriate to do so. It may help you to remember things with images, events and things from your own life and experiences;

4) Do mind-maps of what you know, if you do not know what mind-maps are, get online and look at Tony Buzan's work on mindmaps. I think you will have more fun drawing them than doing them on a computer but that is your call. There is loads of software out there and much of it free;

5) Sing it! Yes sing it out loud in the bathroom and make it fun. Have conversations with yourself aloud whilst you bathe about the topic.

Sanguine Decision Making

A decision! Oh I love to keep my options open! So many possibilities! Yes there are so many possibilities and so many options and sanguines just love to keep those options open. Sanguines feel pressured to keep those options open and have strong reactions against being boxed in. Combine this with being unbelievably optimistic it is not a small wonder that things invariably get left for the last moment. The challenge for the sanguine is to see what is appropriate, for the default reactions, though they often work, will inevitably get you into trouble. If the sanguine is not careful decisions can be delayed until the situation imposes its limits, meaning that the time for options runs out, removing the 'strategic' advantage. The other problem is that the natural optimism, forces one to make the decisions whilst really pressured (Well sanguines thrive on this one!). This will make it difficult to really combine natural creativity with strategic advantage, which further limits the sanguine. Since sanguines do not like to be boxed in we must use this gift. See that keeping one's options open requires some work. If we can act earlier then we can stop the pain of being unnecessarily restricted.

7 Sanguine Steps to Successful Decision Making

1) Talk to yourself about the situation and make a notes preferably in picture stories;

2) Work out what outcomes you would prefer and visualise them. Walk through them and see what the implications are. Keep the picture story notes going. Narrow your preferences down;

3) Walk yourself through your preferences and see how you can keep your options open as much as possible. See the bottlenecks and picture them. Give them interesting funny names. Work out when the time deadlines will arrive for the bottlenecks and what must be done by then;

4) Now you are ready with options and times, you will be freer to be sanguine without tripping yourself up make steps 1 to 3 fun because they are the most difficult to do before the time. The natural tendency is to leave them undone until absolutely necessary but this will box you in and that is precisely what the sanguine does not want;

5) Now hold the essential elements in your

memory and those wonderful pictorial reminders and now hang loose and prepare to be creative and have fun. Remember that the rules are made to be broken and now that you know the rules and bottlenecks you can be free to break them understanding how they entrap or enable you. You can either feel the pain of the least amount of discipline necessary to do the thing or the pain of the circumstances which compel you to do precisely what you do not want to do. Dealing with things in this way saves you the undesirable pain and helps you to be a better sanguine at being sanguine;

6) Be relaxed and make things as much fun as possible. Be really creative and unpredictable and have loads of fun doing it;

7) Make the decision expecting the outcome but see what you can squeeze out of the decision making, more flexibility, more fun, more enjoyment.

Sanguines tend to make decisions based upon people and the circumstances around them. The journey is infinitely more interesting than the goal. So do what you do in a way that makes the journey interesting and people centred. Do not allow the goal oriented types to squeeze you into their moulds unnecessarily but remember that there are those times when it is appropriate to adopt the natural strategies of the other types, learning to find that balance and to clearly grasp what is appropriate is perhaps the most difficult of lessons for all types to learn; it however is the path that leads to wisdom. Know that you will make many mistakes, so do not cry too long over them (Do I really need to say this to a sanguine?). Those mistakes, the lessons and the striving to learn the lessons from the mistakes, is that steep path to wisdom, be gentle with yourself and know that what may seem firm and certain at the time, may become clearly something which is no longer the fixed 'fact' that you thought you had grasped, do not worry about this, it is essential to learning, study and the journey through life, just be gentle with yourself and be open to change; everything around you is in transformation and so are you, relax and accept it. Good luck and have fun!

Sanguine Communication

Like the old bards, sanguines stories will always change according to the circumstances. The thousand line epic poems were probably composed by a sanguine and I can imagine a melancholic historian fixing the story of the poem firmly after much research into a recorded poem that the sanguine probably managed to tell in almost the same way less than ten times out of the thousand times it was recited! The broad point being shared and the details, were made to serve the effect of the story. Why on earth try to pin it down. The reactions to the story are like a dance and the dance is not made to be choreographed but to express an impression of the event in as colourful a manner as can be mustered. Why on earth would anyone tell a dry and boring old story, full of facts but utterly uninteresting? When we are accused of stretching the truth (if we stick to the exact details of the event at all) they completely miss the point! Is not the point to entertain? The problem is that the other types may not share your point of view (in fact they do not) and though they will find it entertaining the 'facts' tend to be important to them. The difficult art of narrating the events of our lives imaginatively, entertainingly and with lots of audience reactions is best served up by holding to the key facts, especially when some of your audience may have been present and beginning to wonder if they were part of the same event that you are narrating. Which of course you can deny. The melancholic will almost always feel the need to correct the details unless you overwhelm them, for 'facts' are really important to them and if you continue, at some point they will make you pay and melancholics have memories like elephants! They are the natural historians! Whilst phlegmatics will view you with an inscrutable amusement and they too tend to have memories like elephants. The choleric will enjoy it, if they are in the mood for entertainment. If however the choleric is not in the mood for entertainment they will want you to get to the point and will perhaps interrupt in frustration, they want you to get to the point and move on.

Four Points to Succesful Communication

1) Learn to read the audience intuitively to decide what is appropriate, since this is a part of your natural genius anyway, just persevere you will get better at it;

2) Resist your natural tendency to launch into a story before reading where the audience is. When you get better at it you can work it out whilst telling a story, perhaps to judge from the reactions of the audience, but resist this in the beginning until you become fairly adept at 'reading the audience';

3) Stay true to the key facts whilst you spice up the story, practice spicing up what really happened rather than the possible trajectories of the story, this takes alot more skill, and the mastery you gain will make you much more entertaining in the long run without upsetting the sensibilities of some of the audience. It's a long journey though and will take time, so be gentle with yourself and just keep trying over time small gradual changes have a large collective effect.

4) When communicating with different types remember that they have strengths:

a) Melancholics will list the facts and the reasons;

b) Phlegmatics will tend to say only what they think is necessary and will do so in a laid back non-intrusive manner with appropriate and acute observations and will tend to make an effort not to offend;

c) Cholerics want to get to the point, quickly. They usually do not want to waste time and want to achieve something, they care less about the facts and more about what they are trying to achieve in the moment but the facts still manage to be important to them insofar as they serve whichever goal they are driving at.

This gives you three other ways of telling the story. When trying to convince these types reflect their styles as it is natural to them and they won't have to interpret what you are saying into their mode as you are telling the story. It gets rid of a layer for them and this makes your job easier. The acute observation of the phlegmatic can make an inescapable point that shows the quarry that you have been watching the matter for a long time and have grasped the pattern well. Whilst the listing of facts as the melancholic very quickly gets the point over but avoid their tendency to specialised language and hold to your strength of getting the story understood. The choleric eye on the goal approach is incredibly useful but be careful of their no prisoners approach to communication save when it is absolutely appropriate. At all times depend upon and refine you natural genius of intuition, feel the state of your audience and learn to respond appropriately to the changes. You will end up being a much better communicator for it, remember improvement of these skills will always be a work in progress.

Silence

Remember there are times when silence is golden. Learn to use it and resist your tendency to impulsively fill silences. You will discover that silence can at times achieve that which speech cannot and at other time silence will achieve what much speech will have to work hard to do. This is a difficult one for a sanguine and tends to take a long time to learn but persevere, it is worth alot more than you can imagine. Most of all it lets others speak, and how best to learn where someone is but from their own mouths. This skill most of all will help you to overcome one of the greatest complaints of all types about sanguines, which is that sanguines talk so much that no one else gets a chance to say anything (observing phlegmatics is a great help with this one). This will save you from the danger of assuming that everyone agrees with you when in fact they do not but never got a chance to say.

Remember that your great sanguine strength is communication, so enjoy it but work at making it oh so much better. Like the bard you will master the art of keeping your audience enraptured, enthralled and eating from your hands like babies. If one must be the centre of attention then let us be the best we can be at it!

Sanguine Alone

Alone! Oh no! This is not the strength of a sanguine. Being alone can be a draining and difficult experience for a sanguine. Imagine being stranded on a desert island with everything you love but utterly alone, with no one to speak to and no company at all. Whilst this may be seen as heaven by a melancholic and possibly a phlegmatic it is the vision of hell for a pure sanguine. Why would anyone wish to do that to themselves. Being alone is usually draining for sanguines and cholerics but this does not necessarily have to be the case. There are two main things that sanguines find difficult that are usually associated with being alone; lack of activity and lack of stimulation. Without being careful it is possible to find oneself chasing one's tail in a never ending circle of meaningless activity and this will leave one feeling overwhelmed, stressed and eventually depressed. Some time being alone will allow one to reflect, reassess and realign and protect you from this very common error.

Eight Uses of Being Alone

The reasons that being alone is a really beneficial thing to do. They are:

1) It allows you to reflect;

2) It allows you to unwind and throw off the influence of the day's events and the influence of others, helping you to clear your mind;

3) It helps to strengthen your independence;

4) It gets rid of stress;

5) It lifts the spirits;

6) It allows you to reassess your life path;

7) It allows you to realign your activities;

8) It keeps you on track in your life.

Sanguines find it easier to be alone whilst doing something. Walking out or jogging in nature whether it be in a park, in open spaces or through a wooded area will be alot easier to do than sitting alone. Environments dominated by greens - plants - and blues - large bodies of water - are very relaxing and renewing. Staring into a fire is also renewing for a sanguine. Swimming is another activity that makes it easier to be alone. Gardening is another important activity to consider. It takes at least twenty minutes for the mind to really unwind and begin to release its fixation with the activities of our days. For a sanguine being alone can be combined with exercise.

Alone Activities for Sanguines

1) Long interesting walks or jogs in nature;

2) Swimming;

3) Tai Chi, bagua, yoga;

4) Gardening;

5) Birdwatching;

6) Painting, photography and or arts and crafts;

7) Use your imagination as you have bucket-loads of it.

As with everything that is difficult it is better to build up the times we engage in them gradually. Avoid the sanguine tendency to be so enthusiastic that you run out of steam, because of the burden of doing too much, much too soon. Being optimistic has its positives, but this is a definite downside. Be gentle with yourself and build up the times that you involve in these activities. Begin with twenty minutes and build up gradually, when you want to increase the times hold back and reward your regularity after perhaps a fortnight or a month by increasing the times by five or ten minutes. It will allow this activity to become an established habit. If you are a sanguine that manages to do these kinds of activities regularly then I think you know exactly what I am talking about. Reward yourself occasionally perhaps every fortnight or month by spending as long as you like at the activity of your choice but avoid exhausting yourself so utterly that it becomes impossible to continue with your established routine (Oh dear! This is the worse word a sanguine can think of! I have used the dreaded R word, 'Routine!'. Fortunately or unfortunately it does have a necessary place in our lives. Think of it as essential maintenance.)

Sanguine Unwell

Like all hot types sanguines hate being unwell. If being unwell means that we have to spend time being still, unable to keep moving or to communicate then this is even worse. The prospect of having to eat or drink medicines or foods that we do not like makes it even a more depressing prospect. Just imagine what it must be like for someone saddled with looking after you. Your stories can turn into whingeing, constantly changing your mind, restlessness, becoming an absolute busybody and intruding into everyone's lives or abject depression at the prospect of being prisoner. All sanguines, save the sanguine melancholic, do not like to dwell on being unwell so I will not.

Nine Ways to Make the Experience of Being Unwell More Interesting

1) Look out of a window and allow yourself to daydream;

2) Try painting or art if you can manage it;

3) Listen to an audio book;

4) Listen to music, perhaps a compilation of music that brings back wonderful memories;

5) Daydream;

6) Tell stories that allow you to really explore your imagination without restriction, if you can manage;

7) Sleep, sleep and sleep;

8) Get more sleep;

9) Have as many visits from old friends as you can and be as dramatic as you can in ensuring the repeat visits of those visits you really enjoy;

That is it. I will say no more, enough on this topic.

Sanguine Impulses

You are all or nothing. Passionate about what you do. You hate to be restricted and wish to always plunge into things, save where life's lessons have taught you that caution is the best policy, but that would have to be a very difficult lesson indeed. The sanguine plunges, immerses and tastes; this is their genius. Being drawn to the experience of immersion of total experiences is the sanguine way and with great stamina you will plunge repeatedly into the activity whilst truly savouring the experience. This sensuous way is the sanguine secret so do not be tempted to give it up for anything. The lesson is to remember that you may immerse yourself without taking the time to grasp what you are immersing yourself into. Be very careful of first impressions, for your tendency to plunge may take you into a raging torrent that you mistook for a calm and easy lake. Whilst you like a challenge and may enjoy living on the edge, just learn the restraint that allows you to understand what you are getting yourself into. Then you can ensure that you have the resources, both of body and spirit as well as whatever other resources may be needed. Failing to do this is a popular sanguine weakness. The natural courage, stamina and passion must learn the quality of sagacity, which is derived from the Latin for sage meaning the wise. By wisdom you will learn when to commit and when to withhold, when to speak and when to be silent, when to plunge and when to watch patiently and when to fight and when to make peace. This is a test that each type faces but you view and approach this test from your very own sanguine standpoint. This is the Divine gift to sanguines, for if each type faced the same test from identical standpoints, the world would be in pale monochrome and a boring place indeed. Sanguines more than any other type love variety, so what a gift variety of standpoints is. Just remember this point when you become irritated with someone entrenched in a position or standpoint that you find particularly infuriating. The skill learned in learning to empathise with them, even mastering how to help them to see other perspectives or just accepting their standpoint as it is, will serve you well and give benefits way in excess of the difficulty of mastering this difficult skill.

Your creative impulse and taste for change will mean that often you move on much too early to enjoy the fruits of your labour. Learning the gift of sagacity will help to teach you to know when to act and will endow you with the discipline. But remember that human beings are not meant to be isolated, we are social creatures and so learn to surround yourself with companions that you can trust and who have strengths in these areas. Strengthen yourself with companions of all types, live well with them and benefit from their counsel. They like you, will sometimes get it wrong and that in itself is a lesson. Remember that people are what they are, learn their patterns and accept them for what they are. When things in relationships go wrong accept it as a lesson and use the lesson well. The sanguine disposition in many of these cases is to take the hurt deeply since sanguines expect the others to commit with the same abandon and generosity of spirit as themselves. Accept that this just may not be their gift and learn to accept the gifts they have to offer whilst not expecting the ones that they may not possess. Avoid idealism. Things are as they are and your opinion of what they should be is irrelevant. The more you expect the world to conform to your idealistic presumptions the more disappointments there will be, the more pain you will suffer and the less you will learn about the way things truly are. Your idealistic presumptions will definitely teach you about your own worldview and give you an opportunity to give it up as you journey to witnessing things as they really are. And what a gift that truly is, to see things with clarity and to surrender to the way things truly are. Sanguine dreams are in need of this lesson and they share this need especially with melancholics but for very different reasons.

As a sanguine you wish to get close to things with your intuitive sensuousness in order to grasp them intimately. This is your genius. Whilst some types will count, expecting knowledge of things to have discrete parts the sanguine seems to want to feel the tides, eddies and textures of things; to taste them and experience them deeply. When this comes out it may sound a little fuzzy but persevere and learn how to express these things in a language of feeling. Once you have mastered this then learn how to express it in terms that the other types may understand. Rome was not built in a day and this skill will take time and much work. Be patient with yourself and time. Work with yourself not against it, you are the greatest gift that you have to use.

Though you love change, you hate to be contained and will feel pressure to keep your options open, learn how to keep them open and to know when committing actually keeps the options most flexible for you in the broader scheme of things. When you are hemmed in it will tend to feel claustrophobic, distinguish between your fears and anxieties and what truly hems you in. Anxiety has a connection to the breath so when you are anxious breathe slowly and deeply into your belly, walk around, look around and sometimes look into your heart, actually look into your heart turning your eyes down whilst breathing deeply. Concentrate on your breath and just wait the anxiety out, the nauseous constricted feeling in your belly may not go away but it will relax somewhat and will become less able to snatch away your judgement. The art of making balanced judgements is a journey and we can with steady work only become better at it.Since your element is wind you need to change direction, race, slowly caress the ground, rise up to heights, swoop down and turn and twist like the wind. You and the wind are different expressions of the same fundamental elemental energetic pattern. Use your nature to explore and delight in life and activities. But like the wind learn when to lie still, when to rage like a hurricane and when to slip unnoticed across the earth.

You may find that you are more fixated upon the outside of things, you see the form, detail and the texture first before you perceive meaning and what is in the depths. Patient playful exploration of the outsides of things will lead you to meaning unlike some other types who first seem to start with meaning and then become fixated upon form and the outsides of things. Use your genius and learn to ride her well, do not think yourself any less because of your natural disposition. Study your natural disposition and use it well. You begin with the senses whilst others begin with the 'facts'(whatever they are!) and thought. They journey from the inside out whilst you journey from the outside in, both are valid and they both have their strengths. Twist turn and playfully explore. Your genius is made to work that way.

Summary

Now this completes our journey through the amazing creature that is the pure sanguine. I hope that you have gained some insights and tools, that you can use to help you on the journey to being a better you. I think you have understood that the sanguine like all types possesses strengths and weaknesses. Strengths may become weaknesses when they are used inappropriately, often because there is a failure to consider context and what that consequently requires. Weaknesses may become strengths when they are used appropriately, taking consideration of the the context and the requirements. In order to do this we must develop wisdom and the ability to keep working at the skills which are needed to respond appropriately to events in the world, because the sanguine is as changeable as the wind, we need to keep our journey interesting, varied and fun because sanguines find routines and monotony very difficult to deal with. Making things fun, interesting and varied keeps an eye on enjoying the process of doing the thing. This is an approach that will help to keep the sanguine interested and engaged in what they are doing. The lesson is to work with the way that you are and do not assume that there is something wrong with the patterns that make you, you. You are wired the way that you are, so learn to use the self that you have well. There will be lots of mistakes and failures but use them to learn. Study the way things go wrong and the way they go right. Use that knowledge to become better at working with yourself. Despite this do not make excuses for yourself when you have done something really badly, utterly inappropriate and downright stupid. Accept responsibility for your part in making that happen, but study it. Study your errors. Study your successes and learn how to increase your successes and reduce your errors. There will always be errors. Self development ends at death and until then the ball is still in your court. So play ball and let us practice using ourselves well, we owe it to ourselves.

Having completed our journey through the almost pure sanguine, it is time to take a look at the specific mixtures. God willing, I am sure you will find your specific mixture in one of them. It may be the time to take a break, before proceeding. Thank you for taking the time to get this far with me and I hope that it has been a rewarding and enriching experience, but now wait until you see the mixtures! I believe it will be even more fun.

THE MIXES

In our makeup there are at least three main contributing aspects of our personalities. They all come together to make us what we are. So, despite all our amazing similarities we each remain a unique differentiated individual. Know that even if you choose to imitate someone, only you can possibly imitate them in the way that you do. You cannot escape your own individuality, the best option you have is to explore it and become comfortable with it. Your individuality cannot be sold to you with some mass produced brand, or other mass activity. In fact the thought is itself an absurdity. Since you are already an individual then the very best thing you can do is to explore the way in which you are already differentiated or made different. Your capacity to use what you already have will unfold that individuality in a way that is useful to you, those around you and your community as a whole.

What Makes You, YOU?

From your parents you receive your unique genetic material and bodily energetic nature, you were formed as an egg whilst your mother was an embryo in her mother. Miraculously three generations of your family were present in your maternal grandmother. As your maternal grandmother's food, experiences and context was becoming her, it was also becoming you. So your mother links you back to your maternal grandmother, in whom the egg that would become you was formed! This egg and the sperm of your father forms the zygote that began you as a unique event combining the seed essence of both your mother and father. This begins the formation of the body and will form the basic foundation of your bodily nature, which is in no way separate from your psychological nature.

At the time of the quickening – between sixteen to twenty weeks – in embryonic development the soul is blown into the embryonic body. This soul contributes the bulk of our psychological nature and must now fuse with and make use of the body. It enters at the heart and then must differentiate its faculties into the functional organs, fusing with the body and governing it. From now on until death there will be such an intimate energetic exchange between the two, making it pointless to refer to them as separate entities. They are for all intents and purposes one, until the soul separates from the body at death; and even then it will not be truly separate. At the end of its life within the body the soul will inherit all the acquired knowledges and experiences. What must always be remembered is that the soul possesses a body and that it is not the body that possesses a soul. The soul governs and the lack of recognition of this fundamental reality and failure to shape one's life according to this realisation will make you psychologically and physically imbalanced and eventually unwell.

All of your experiences, your language, your social context, family, parents, education, work and other factors, will all contribute to shaping you. In order to be in the world and make sense of it you will construct a narrative or story of your being in the world, that will shape the way you see it. These experiences will also shape our emotional and energetic temperament which is changeable within limits.

The combination of the three components – body, soul and narrative self – makes you what you are. The bodily nature may be cool and slow whilst the spirit is hot and quick and depending upon your state of health you will express this combination differently throughout your life, however, there is a form that is set and that can only be transformed within the form's natural limits. It is this fusion of body, spirit and developed narrative self that makes you, YOU. What we are examining is this fusion expressed in your psychological nature.

As a sanguine you will broadly express your psychological nature in one of three ways.

The Sanguine Forest

The mixes are as follows:

Choleric Sanguine - This is a sanguine with strong choleric qualities, in other words this is a commanding active goal-oriented sanguine;

Melancholic Sanguine - This is a sanguine with strong melancholic qualities, it is also the most difficult sanguine form to master. This sanguine may seem bipolar, seeming melancholic at times and sanguine at others;

Phlegmatic Sanguine - This is a sanguine with phlegmatic qualities, this form hates to be contained with a vengeance. These are incredibly intuitive sanguines.

Since we are all a mixture of the four elements we possess a primary personality type within which the others are expressed. However, two personality traits will usually be most dominant. The way that I understand this is that one element provides a seat for the others, whilst the secondary type is the second most expressed of the personality traits. All the primary sanguine types will have a tendency to be very communicative, changeable, creative, expressive and intuitive.

Using the analogy of a forest, in the sanguine forest, you will see mainly three types of trees, expressing their differing shapes, sizes and adaptation to their specific contexts. So there will be an infinite variety of sanguines, but they will all conform to three main patterns. However, rarely, very very very rarely, you will encounter a sanguine in whom it seems that very very very little of the other personality traits are expressed, and when you see that then know that you have found an incredibly rare occurrence indeed.

The Uniqueness of Each One of Us

You will see that there is such variety. In fact, due to the constant change of the narrative self and the maintenance of the body's health, the job of becoming you is constantly in process. Within your boundaries there is endless change. Self development must be an inseparable and constant aspect of our lives if we are to actively take on the implications and responsibilities of being human beings. We are actively expressing and honing our uniqueness by taking on the task of self development. By removing excrescences, throwing out rubbish, building on undeveloped foundations, polishing and constantly working on our expression of being human for our brief passage through the world, we become better persons. Because time is limited we must make use of it. And the only possession we truly have for the journey is ourselves. You will only happen once. You will not be repeated. As every leaf on a tree is different, every raindrop, every pebble, every ant; as everything is different so are you an utterly unique occurrence that will never, ever be repeated.

The Master and the Servant

Your main or primary personality trait I call the master. Your master characterises what you are and it makes use of your secondary trait which I call the servant, because the master makes use of its servant trait to express its impulses. So a sanguine-choleric is a sanguine with choleric traits. Put simply, the sanguine-choleric makes use of choleric aspects to be sanguine. They will use choleric tactics to fulfill a sanguine strategy. The phlegmatic and melancholic traits we possess will also serve the sanguine strategies of the sanguine, but will usually be overshadowed by the master-servant psychological nature which we should be able to recognise fairly easily once we know how to do so. By making use of our selves and dealing with others according to their natures, we can make life so much easier. Developing these other traits in ourselves is usually a little more difficult than the Master-Servant traits, but with application and hard work it is very possible and this can often contribute to us becoming more balanced human beings.

4 Ways to be Sanguine

So there are four ways to be sanguine:

1) The Pure Sanguine – rare and is in reality an impossibility since we all carry the four elements within us. So when we speak of the

pure sanguine, we are speaking about a sanguine in whom the other three elements are very weakly expressed;

2) The Sanguine-Choleric;

3) The Sanguine-Melancholic;

4) and the Sanguine-Phlegmatic.

Summary

Now we will begin the journey into the three main mixtures that make up the Sanguine forest. By now I am sure you appreciate the vast variety that you will find within each of these subtypes. Human beings are simply amazing creatures and what a pleasure it is to be able to observe ourselves.

THE SANGUINE-MELANCHOLIC

The sanguine-melancholic is a wonder. It is a type that has tremendous possibilities, containing the capacity to express all of the temperaments in a very balanced manner. It combines two very opposite types with great similarities. Their combination aids the expression of the others, but with great capacity comes a great test. I call this type a 'non-complementary mixture'. Earth and air really do not mix well. It is either earth or air and that is the problem with this type, making it very difficult to master, rather like a deep ocean fraught with great danger. The sanguine-melancholic has to work hard to master this form, but with perseverance the payoffs are huge. The sanguine-melancholic can appear almost bipolar, for the two aspects of the personality type, tend to express themselves very distinctly and mustering an appropriate response is a difficult job, requiring much will, practice and patience.

This is a sanguine who is able to muster melancholic

thought to fulfill sanguine strategies. They are incredibly creative, able to think on the fly and will produce non-fuzzy water tight rational arguments. They may be a little random at times but this sanguine is loved for the rigour of their thinking. They will tend to seem organised but those who know them, grow to expect a sanguine. The constitution is strong and they love food, variety and all the things that a sanguine loves. If you see a sanguine producing melancholic arguments and traits consistently, but whose strategies are clearly sanguine then you have found the sanguine-melancholic, however if you find that the strategies are melancholic but they employ sanguine tactics to fulfill their goals then you are dealing with a melancholic-sanguine who is another non-complementary type being very different to the sanguine-melancholic.

The World According to the Sanguine-Melancholic

CV

I am intuitive, fun loving and talkative. My confident, friendly and open demeanour makes me very popular and my sanguine easygoing nature attracts everyone and so I will usually have an extensive and impressive contact list. I can think and set things into goal oriented lists but am always more interested in feelings and the journey rather than the goals. For that reason I will tend to come up with wonderful plans that make sense, however, if they do not feel right I will tend to abandon them since I may become very uncomfortable. This often earns me the reputation of being unreliable and can make me difficult to work with. However, once a thing feels right and I can commit to it the journey is guaranteed to be enjoyable and I will make it my personal mission to increase the fun. Like all sanguines, I am as changeable as the wind but will always have an excellent well reasoned argument as to why, and can sometimes make life difficult even for myself to work with because of this trait.

I am a great peoples' person and can convey ideas very well. My communication is loaded with anecdotes and jokes. I move on quickly and unlike the melancholic-sanguine am not easily offended. As a creative person I bridge the gap between the process oriented ones who see the world by feelings, people and values, and the goal oriented ones who see the world by reasons, objectives and principles. Having me around in such circumstances can save a lot of communication time as long as I do not launch myself into a prolonged story, full of anecdotes, becoming so interested in stealing the stage without regard for what has to be done. I make sense, notice connections, help to complete plans with astounding ideas and insights and tend to tip the creative balance into the direction of success.

The Sanguine-Melancholic Traits According to the World

You are thinkers and really fun to be with. We trust you easily and find it easy to speak to you, since your conversation is always peppered with insights, interesting facts, quotes and observations. It makes conversation not only easy, but intensely stimulating. You are compassionate, easygoing and generous, as a result we thoroughly enjoy your company, conversation and advice. You tend to think things through which makes you an asset.

You are an amazing door opener, opening situations and opportunities that others would think impossible. Your enthusiastic optimism, sanguine creativity, mental dexterity and persuasive arguments seem to crack open gems hidden in boulders so big that many of us would not even bother, but you can get in there and open it all up. The only problem we have is that you will sometimes promise the impossible and convince the world – especially yourself – that it is probable, landing us in some real fixes. You are natural salesmen and women, please, please only sell what is there! Your tendency to sell potential leaves us scratching our heads and working overtime to utilise the potentialities that things should have but which we have never tested. The less said about this, the better!

We do have some more complaints. You may come up with ideas or consider ideas, discuss them and agree to them and their courses of action. When everyone has committed you can suddenly change your mind and without informing anyone, change your course of action. At these times it makes it incredibly difficult to plan around you and it takes a long time to figure this aspect of you out. It seems that, though you may discuss and like the idea in the moment, your feelings about it are much more important to you than the plans, discussions and ideas and you may tend to just change your mind leaving us all in limbo. It is as if in one moment you are a raving melancholic and then suddenly you decide to switch to sanguine mode. We just do not know which end of the sanguine-melancholic we are due to get, which makes it a little like playing russian roulette.

You tend to avoid confrontations like the plague and will employ the sanguine ostrich tactic of burying your head in the sand in the belief that the problems will go away, despite clearly knowing that it will not. Many elaborate discussions and activities turn out to be your avoidance of conflict in hindsight. Please do appreciate that this is incredibly confusing.

You do not like to be contained and feel pressure to keep your options open. This can become mixed with melancholic procrastination and sanguine avoidance tactics, which is one of the most infuriating experiences for us to work through. Waiting for the possibility of perfection and not wanting to be committed can come together in very disastrous ways and then your sanguine disposition makes it very difficult to be angry with you. Eventually some of us just run away.

The Sanguine-Melancholic Impulses

You exist to create. You stand at the lip of the abyss, straddling the expanse to make things manifest in the world. You stand there as a puzzle-maker, drawing the paths of potentiality into manifestation. You will even inspire, but you love this standpoint intensely and the journey into the world of manifestation can be a very difficult one. Problem solving, seeing potential, creativity, communication and openhandedness characterise you. You will walk back and forth within this interspace of potentiality and actualisation; walking between these two worlds without becoming attached to the manifestations. You will remain interested only as long as creativity and unfolding potentiality remain dominant; beyond this point you will tend to lose interest and motivation. The journey through the zone of manifesting potential is difficult for you. With discipline and training mastery is possible, but this is not a zone you will tend to enter comfortably and you will have to work to continue through this zone. You walk the interspace and are a natural master of it. You naturally need a team that can take care of manifesting and making sound the implementation of the potential in the world, in a way that ensures that you benefit. If you remain alone it would be wise to ensure that your part remains in the zone of your mastery. Other than this perhaps you should avoid venturing beyond this stage, whilst ensuring that any remuneration or benefits that you need or desire are given to you for your mastery. Remember, due to your natural generosity you tend not to see your involvement in terms of your individual benefit. You must learn the rules and ways of ensuring that your involvement brings you benefit and that your reward is given to you. Unless you do this you stand the risk of being abused, with very little reward or appreciation.In relationships, you love and give generously bending over backwards without seeing into the future implications. You will tend to make many excuses for those around you and to be incredibly generous to them. You will optimistically argue against your suspicions and will use your melancholic arguments to convince yourself of your optimistic assessments of others. This is your default and cannot be helped, however what you must do, is learn from your experiences and adjust your responses to ensure that you protect your position. People are the way they are and you cannot force them to correspond with your optimistic assessment of them so when they disappoint you, and some of them necessarily will, ensure that you have provided some protection of your position and are able to ensure some measure of good behaviour on their part by having kept some to the chips firmly under your control. Be careful of promising too much, because as a result of your sanguine nature, you will be forced to find ways of slipping out of impossible commitments.

You have a tendency to exhaust yourself, for creativity seems to possess its own natural rhythm - but beware! Your form needs energy in order to bridge this incredible gulf. Yes, your mastery takes energy. Though you may hate it, routine is the only way that you will be able to make use of your potential whilst being able to continue to do what you are best at. With routine and life balance you will find that you are able keep going. This form is prone to lots of crashes due to overextending itself. Learning to overcome this natural tendency is a sign that you are on the right track.

Summary

The melancholic sanguine form is one of the 'non-complementary' forms which is difficult to master, but which possesses incredible capacity. Essentially, we have a creative, problem solver with persuasive communication skills. The natural strength of this type is not in working through detail but in initiating and finding a way to make things happen. This form is an incredibly generous one and needs to ensure that it protects its generous nature so that it balances its selfless generosity with the worldly necessity of rewards in order to be able to make its way in the world. In relationships this type must be careful of excessive optimism about people without ensuring that it secures its interests. They must ensure that their essential interests are at least taken care of. To unleash the incredible potential of this form you will need to work hard at it.

THE SANGUINE-CHOLERIC

The sanguine-choleric is an active, busy and communicative type. This is a communicative type with a strong impulsive nature. The combination of two hot types results in someone who is restless and forever feels compelled to be busy. This 'complementary mixture' brings together the flexibility, creativity and changing interests of the sanguine, which is enabled to employ the focused, goal oriented and driven nature of the choleric. This is a sanguine who can be goal oriented and a serial achiever but needs variety to keep their changing sanguine nature satisfied. The complementary nature of the mixture means that they are consistent in their nature. You will not get the bi-polar changeability of the sanguine-melancholic. Wind and fire mix to create a hot, tornado like mixture; hot, raging, moving, changing and incredibly difficult to pin down. To harness the power of this mixture you must submit to its hot and changeable nature. It is fundamental to the type and its strongest aspect - so why waste it? This type pushes through obstacles, racing around them and trying all of the changeable strategies of the sanguine but will often refuse to take any prisoners. If you are with them they are intensely loyal, but if they are against you be careful! In the heat of the moment we miss things and this type will have a tendency to be hasty and will hence fail to notice many things, but this is counterbalanced by the knack of knowing just what is needed.

The World According to the Sanguine-Choleric

I am fun, conversation loving and cannot be still, and am at my best in busy engaging active environments with lots of change, stimulation and challenges. I am naturally an active creative person that will ceaselessly approach problems from multiple angles. Imagine me as a turning, twisting wind that drills, hammers, pushes, pulls, whirls, twirls and constantly explores the objects of my interest. There will always necessarily be objects of my interest, because of the sanguine bane of boredom when stimulation is in short supply. However, I am the sanguine that will overturn the apple cart in search of something to stimulate me, employing all manner of strategies in pursuit of my interest. I simply love to be actively engaged. In the arenas of my varied interests you will find that I have excelled, handling workloads that others would baulk at, but on the other hand I will move on to the other project with relative ease and an eerie lack of connection to what I have just left behind. Others tend to find this a little frightening. When I have moved on, I have moved on - that is just the way it is! My stamina is legendary. Once committed I can keep going when others are flagging and will manage to express an infectious enthusiasm whilst enjoying the process of the journey. You can guarantee that I will have fun along the way, whilst being utterly goal directed. This may all be incredibly exhausting.If you get into my way do not be surprised if I bulldoze, evade, circumvent and twist my way around you. It is nothing personal and most likely there is no malice. I need to get past you and am not an incredibly reflective type. I know by doing and will explore my options in action without sometimes being completely aware of my next moves. What I do is seldom premeditated and malicious. My objective is to get past you and onto the next goal and that is just the way I am wired. Of course some things will happen that perhaps I should not have done but I will tend to realise this long after the event and may be a little too proud to admit it. You will know that I am repentant by the change in the way I treat you, tending to make amends a while after the event.

I see form, texture and structure first, and will move from this to meanings. This makes me a very good creative and a subtle 'designer'. My creativity is ever changing, focused and active.If these are the qualities that you want to be around, then I am your person but I do not do boring. In order to win I will keep going, quickly abandoning winning if it loses its appeal to me.

The Sanguine Choleric According to the World

You are really fun to speak to, possess an agile and changeable mind and consequently make very interesting and exciting conversation. You never stop talking! Your presence, positivity and drive is fun and can draw us out of our deepest depression, however you can be exhausting since you keep going and going. Since you are a natural busybody, once you become fixated upon a thing or a person then that person is really in trouble, for you can be inescapable and unrelenting.

You drive projects forward with energy, resourcefulness and variation, grabbing what is at hand with an astounding intuition and intent. Your energy is boundless and your very presence can feel like a tornado. Things change when you are around whether we would like them to or not. Dealing with you by confronting you head on is too difficult a prospect once you have decided upon your direction; there is no stopping you. For us to deal with you head on when we disagree is not a palatable option. We are forced to avoid, go around and not commit to you or your direction; we have to deal with you in a phlegmatic manner. We will however face your fury for this and very few - save some of the phlegmatic types - dare venture into this ground. Dealing with you under these circumstances requires the development of avoidance into a very fine art.

You make things happen, hold situations together and

bring change, creativity and fun. We love you, but are naturally apprehensive when our opinions and intended paths are at divergence with yours.

The Sanguine-Choleric Impulses

You stand upon the lip of the abyss of potentialities, striding forth into the world of actualities; bustling back and forth stridently, preferring the abyss but daring to stride into the world in order to manifest the potentiality. The one thing that must be said is that it must happen quickly. However your natural standpoint is this bustling between these two worlds and this interface is absolutely your zone. Your hot nature causes you to drive to swift outcomes as you twist, turn, badger and drive the situation on. Your natural disposition for knowing by doing and saying often gets you into trouble but this is how you know and do. Actualising is your means of exploring your inner world. You will often put your foot in it and get things wrong but your capacity for quickly and deftly changing direction means that you are a swift learner and will drive towards success in a searching and probing manner. Your intuition is strong, swift and certain. When it begins to wane this is probably a sign that you need rest or are within a zone about which you have serious doubts; perhaps it is time to realign.

Summary

The sanguine-choleric is a very active, busy, talkative and impulsive type. Their whole nature is hot, active and driven. They must be busy. They love to communicate as all sanguines do, however this type, is commanding, impulsive and talkative. They can be wonderful to be around but they have a tendency to make you their project. This type will tell you their life story in five minutes and you will love them for it. They organise, actualise and mobilise. The creativity of this sanguine will be constantly driven towards goals.

THE SANGUINE-PHLEGMATIC

D o not try to pin me down. I am like wind and water, slipping between your fingers, twisting and spinning out of the reach of mountains - like the wind I shed my waters and weight to rise high above. I do not like to be contained and will not be contained. The strategies of the sanguine and the phlegmatic are smoothly and consistently combined within me.

The World According to the Sanguine - Phlegmatic

Forget pinning me down I do not like to commit and need to keep my options open.

Like the wind and the waters, I am flexible and so will move smoothly and deftly around as I act in the world, reacting very badly to restriction. Though you may enjoy my company, conversations and creative abilities please recognise that you cannot pin me down. Your attempts to reign me in, in order to render me comfortable for your own use without destroying my very soul and impulse will not work. I am flexible, moving, taking the shape of many situations in a chameleon like manner and will remain so. I intuitively know what to do and will do what I see is necessary for the situation, then feel the need to move on. What I subjectively perceive really governs me and I am not at all goal oriented. I really do not care about them very much. The journey rather than the goals remains ever so much more important to me. My intuitive insight and love of connecting people in order to subtly bringing benefit, is just my way. If I do have a goal it will be connecting people, benefiting them and or remaining unrestricted. These motivations will tend to lie at the core of what will appear to be goals, so that you will find my projects changing frequently to express these underlying motivations. You may find this frustrating if you become fixated upon a form that you think things should appear in. I do not fixate upon the form of things, but am interested in essential natures. I am much more interested in what is really happening below the surface; in what it is really doing rather than how it appears - arriving at this by my strongest asset which is my intuitive capacity.

As a creative I will explore many courses of action, abandoning many as I search for what feels right. When I am healthy my creative exploration may seem ruthless since I care less about the resources expended and much more about the creative journey. If the result does not express the spirit of the project, I will abandon it. It seems contradictory that I am governed by the maxim that it is better to be roughly right than precisely wrong, yet possess this type of creative urge. Much of the time you would believe that I am not doing anything but that would be incorrect, I observe and explore. I tend to know by expression rather than my internal dialogue. My phlegmatic aspect enables me to observe deep and broad patterns and patterned outcomes.

My friends will testify to my deep intuitive nature and capacity to perceive what they need even before they express it. My intuition can appear invasive when you do not want to disclose your deeper feelings and motivations.I hate doing anything that will not be fun and I love doing things that make a real difference to people. Doing things that do not accord with my deep motivations becomes stifling and I will tend to react claustrophobically. Meaning for me is expressed in a people centred manner; it is what makes a difference to people. Whilst meaning may be very different for other types who see projects and goals, I do not naturally tend to see things that way. Hence, if I commit to a project wholeheartedly it will tend to be for vastly different reasons than other types. Since I am more interested in expressing the spirit of the thing, my motivations will change according to the circumstances because I do not tend to see outcomes in the same way.I absolutely do not do routine willingly. Flexibility and the ability to change direction according to the situation is my way. I change plans in the moment. The sun rises and sets at set times and with set patterns, so I recognise that routine is somewhat necessary. Yes, there is an order and constructed nature of things but I prefer to follow my inner tides rather than artificially constructed orders; to connect to the underlying tides and eddies that can be intuited. Unless I am passionate about the things in which I am involved, I will find routine incredibly tedious and will tend not to do it well; if at all.

The Sanguine-Phlegmatic According to the World

You are incredibly intuitive and sensitive. We utterly enjoy your company and conversation. You seem to have an uncanny ability to divine how I feel about things, balancing the ability to communicate actively and to listen remarkably well. Working with you creatively usually results in work that we can all be incredibly proud of. You are intensely original, insightful and utterly unorthodox. You seem to bring this unorthodoxy to all of your relationships and I would describe you as anarchic. It seems that very little manages to contain you.

Though we love the results of working with you, the experience can be much less of a pleasure than you suspect. It seems impossible to pin you down and working with that uncertainty can be difficult. Since you are fixated upon your internal insights and tides, those of us unfortunate enough to be outside of you - which happens to be all of us - suffer the uncertainty of not knowing quite what is going on or what will happen most of the time. Whilst this may be desirable in some cases, in most it certainly is not and this tends to make life difficult for us.

For you, nothing is sacred and your acrid and anarchic sense of humour can tend to get you into trouble. As with all sanguines you will realise what you are saying as you say it or just after you have said it. Putting your foot in it, is an unavoidable sanguine collateral damage. We your friends have to make excuses for you and there are those times when you just do not care. Your humour usually strikes at observed patterns and can uncomfortably expose people. We would ask you to be a little more gentle for though it is funny it can be quite unnerving. Smart, unorthodox, observant and an acrid wit are definitely your traits.

You walk away from situations with a lack of connection that is often unnerving. You seem able to just slip away and to leave things. It is as if you manage to change your skin and leave it all behind.

I've got to say this one. You seem to find it very difficult to grow up and you are a dreamer, an excessive dreamer and when your head is in the clouds bringing you down to planet earth is difficult.

The Sanguine-Phlegmatic Impulses

Dwelling in the abyss

You dwell in the abyss, turning and diving into its depths and riding its tides. You are not unlike a surfer who awaits the waves and rides their power through to the end. You employ phlegmatic patience to fulfill your sanguine imperatives or strategies. You are less interested in making things manifest in the world than solving the problem creatively and enjoying the process. Once this is completed then you tend not to be interested in sticking around. However, whilst exploring a matter of your interest you will patiently explore by feel and intuition, causing the solution to seemingly emerge out of your interaction and experience of its spirit. Whilst some types like to count and measure parts and qualities, you are fixed upon their essence and seem to just know how to grow a solution that expresses surprising balance and beauty. Your manner may be sanguinely communicative but you are perhaps the least noticeable of the sanguines. Though you are fun to be with you tend to draw less attention to yourself. Recognising and manifesting the potentiality out of the abyss is a thing that you do very well, by that expressing the internal coherence, balance and beauty with an unbelievable way. Other types do not tend to understand your tendency to sit or lie still, whilst awaiting the stirring of things, until those eddies can be seized and ridden out of the abyss. This makes you perhaps the most patient of the sanguines.

Summary

This is a very self contained type, being the coldest of the sanguines and a very consistent 'complementary' form. They can walk away from broken relationships and have a surprising capacity to recover. Their sensuous nature is grounded and deeply intuitive, more-so than any of the other sanguine types. They are the most anarchic and adept at maintaining their personal space. Many of their relationships break down because of their partner's desire to contain them. In order to harness their astounding capacity and creativity you must convince them and set aside time to await their acceptance. It is perhaps best to try catching the attention of this type by leaving a few options in their way and by not being too insistent, since they are naturally resistant to coercion and you will not achieve your best results in this way. In relationships do not push them too much, as this does not work well.

PULLING IT ALL TOGETHER

We have examined the sanguine and its three possible expressions. By now you should have had much fun, learnt lots and noticed so much. I also hope that you have begun to develop an intuitive grasp of sanguines and are able to use this information to help yourself be a better sanguine or be better at dealing with sanguines. This journey should continue with the coming books and will be helped by your repeatedly dipping into this little treasure. Being brutally honest with yourself is difficult in the beginning but seems to become easier with time and practice. Let's re-examine the lessons we have learned, but remember that there is alot more detail in the book.

The Lessons

The lessons are very simple:

1) Work with yourself and not against yourself as you only have nothing else to work with; you had better get to know yourself very, very well.

2) Learn about your default reactions, in order to understand what triggers them. Learn how and when to use them. Ensure that you observe when your default reactions are inappropriate.

3) Observe the other types in order to learn when they deal well with situations. Learn from them. It is not a lack of originality to copy and imitate, for only you can imitate in the way that you do. This is how you may increase your arsenal of responses to the differing situations that make up the fabric of life.

4) Observe, observe, observe! Look, look and look! Learn, learn and learn! Change, change and change. The excuse, 'this is just the way I am!' may be fine for a few occasions but, if you cause discomfort or are caused discomfort, the only person that you have the capacity to change is yourself. So get on with changing yourself!

Seeing patterns helps you to predict outcomes but existence is very sophisticated and you WILL get it wrong.

Learn to enjoy getting it wrong and spend time reflecting. Learn the lessons! Without these lessons you will remain ignorant of that which the error brought, so welcome knowledge, change and learning from the gift of your blessed errors.

People are the way they are so expect them to be that way. The one who has to change is you, you just do not have the capacity to compel them to change and if you reflect upon yourself and your own experience of change, you will tend to be more forgiving of the errors of others.

There are so many ways to approach the same problem and so many ways to see the world. There is such a bewildering array of patterned perspectives. Just practice seeing things from someone else's shoes. It teaches empathy and empathy is a capacity that leads to mercy and understanding of others. Practice it. It will make you a better human being.

We by our behaviour are contributing the nature of the world we live in. When we have changed, we should know that the whole universe has changed. Embracing change and responsibility for our actions empowers us to make a difference to our lives and by that to help to change the lives of others; usually for the better. Do not waste your days, be absolutely active.

Putting it into practice

Keep observing the vast and subtle tapestry of yourself and be awake to the differences you make; see what happens and how it happens. Observe the things that trigger your default responses. Make your behaviour the object of study; see the effectiveness of your strategies to change. Strive to respond appropriately to circumstances and events. Work, work and work at yourself, honing your behaviour, this will be an lifelong project. It just never ends!

Releasing Our Stories on the Journey to Reality

See that the implication of the myriad perspectives that we human beings are capable of possessing means that your perspective is not the only way to see events. Your stories of what happened can change in an instant upon the change of single matter which you assumed was absolute fact. This causes you to realise that there are assumptions underlying what you see. The stories you tell are built on these assumptions, so learn to release them when it is clear that they are wrong and remain open to other perspectives. You do not always have to agree with the perspectives of others, it is sometimes enough to grasp why someone sees things as they do; whether you believe them to be right or wrong. We base our behaviour upon our assumptions, so accepting the way that others see things allows us to understand the manner in which they behave and if there is anything to be avoided then we should avoid it. Having recognised why people do what they do and having been caught by the same pattern of behaviour repeatedly, makes it your own fault. Do not willingly and repeatedly walk into unfavourable situations to which you know the outcomes and then blame it upon others. Accept the way things are and work with them not against them. Use the fundamentals of the situation to transform it and abandon attempting to use what you think should be there. The world is as it is and our ideals do not decide the way it is. The way it should be is an ideal, and the way it is, is simply the way it is.

> *He created the heavens and earth with Reality*
> *The Noble Qur'an: Surah Nahl: 3*

Enjoying and Employing Natural Strengths

Enjoy your natural strengths and employ them. Observe the natural strengths of others and study how to use them. Now that is pretty simple in principle but we all know how difficult that will be to put into practice.

The Next Step

If you want to learn more about the other types read:

Know Yourself Choleric - this explores the Choleric and the different choleric mixtures;

Know Yourself Melancholic - this explores the Melancholic and the different melancholic mixtures;

Know Yourself Phlegmatic - this explores the phlegmatic and the different phlegmatic mixtures.

If you want to learn more about the stories we tell and how to prevent yourself being imprisoned by these stories and ideals then read *Telling It as It Is* when it is published hopefully in 2015. Connect to my blog www.alexcarberry.net